art experiences
for little fingers

open-ended art experiences that help young children explore their world!

by
Sherrill B. Flora
&
Linda Standke

illustrated by
Janet Armbrust

Publisher
Key Education Publishing Company, LLC
Minneapolis, Minnesota

CONGRATULATIONS ON YOUR PURCHASE OF A KEY EDUCATION PRODUCT!

The editors at Key Education are former teachers who bring experience, enthusiasm, and quality to each and every product. Thousands of teachers have looked to the staff at Key Education for new and innovative resources to make their work more enjoyable and rewarding. Key Education is committed to developing and publishing educational materials that will assist teachers in building a strong and developmentally appropriate curriculum for young children.

PLAN FOR GREAT TEACHING EXPERIENCES WHEN YOU USE EDUCATIONAL MATERIALS FROM KEY EDUCATION PUBLISHING COMPANY, LLC

Credits
Authors: Sherrill B. Flora
and Linda Standke
Artist: Janet Armbrust
Editors: George C. Flora
Bernadette Baczynski
Cover Design: Mary Claire
Production: Key Education Staff
Cover Photography: © Comstock
© Brand X Pictures
© Comstock
© Rubberball

Key Education welcomes manuscripts and product ideas from teachers.
For a copy of our submission guidelines, please send a self-addressed, stamped envelope to:

Key Education Publishing Company, LLC
Acquisitions Department
9601 Newton Avenue South
Minneapolis, Minnesota 55431

Standard Book Number:1-933052-05-8
Art Experiences for Little Fingers
Copyright © 2005 by Key Education Publishing Company, LLC
Minneapolis, Minnesota 55431

Introduction

who is this book for?

Art Experiences for Little Fingers is a wonderful resource for anyone who lives, works, or plays with young children. Whether you are a parent, an early childhood educator, a child care provider, or even a grandparent, the art experiences found in this easy-to-use book will provide hours of meaningful fun for you and the little ones in your life!

The activities presented in *Art Experiences for Little Fingers* use inexpensive and readily available materials. Most of the items used in these art experiences can be found in your kitchen or school cupboards. On page 6, you will find a list of suggested "readily available materials" that may assist you in stocking your cupboards.

why is art important in early childhood?

All young children need a variety of experiences to help them explore and learn about their world. Art is an essential part of a child's development because it nurtures the child's natural curiosity and imagination. Art allows the child to experiment with textures, colors, shapes, movement, and space, as well as offering experiences that help increase a child's observation skills, fine motor strength, and eye-hand coordination.

Art experiences also promote increased expressive and receptive language skills. Sitting with your own child or with a group of children in an early childhood setting provides perfect opportunities for talking about all of the basic concepts that they are experiencing. For example, ask "How does the playdough feel?" "Are the bubbles big or small?" "Is the finger paint smooth or rough?" "Tell me about your picture." These activities are also powerful tools for increasing a child's vocabulary.

It is important to praise a child's efforts and accomplishments. Self-esteem and self-confidence are bolstered as you comment on the beauty of a finger painting, the clever shape of a playdough sculpture, or how bright the colors are in that scribble picture. Problem-solving skills are also enhanced when a child is allowed to creatively explore art materials. Children will begin asking questions such as; "What will happen if I mix two different colors of paint together?" "How long will it take for this clay to dry?" "What will happen if I add too much water?"

it's the process, not the product!

Children are busy learning through the process and exploration of art! The final product is not what is important. So, let the imagination of your children run wild as they explore, create, and discover more about the world around them with *Art Experiences for Little Fingers*.

contents

Readily Available materials

alum (powdered)
baby lotion
baby shampoo
baking soda
balsa wood
blender
boric acid
bubble wands
bucket
butcher paper
buttermilk
buttons
cake pan (9" x 13")
candy molds
cardboard
card stock
cinnamon
cheese grater
chocolate
    (semi-sweet)
cloth
clothespins
cloves (ground)
colored chalk
construction paper
contact paper
cookie cutters
cookie sheet
cooling rack
cornmeal
cornstarch
corn syrup
cotton balls
cotton swabs
craft sticks
crayons
cream of tartar
cupcake liners

cupcake tin
dish washing
    detergent
dry starch
duct tape
eggshells
electric mixer
empty containers
    margarine
    yogurt
    baby food
    coffee cans
eye droppers
file folders
finger paint paper
flavored gelatin
flour
food coloring
fruit baskets
glitter
glycerin
honey
ice cube trays
instant coffee
instant pudding
liquid starch
liquid tempera paint
iron
ironing board
Ivory Snow Flakes™
    laundry detergent
marbles
margarine
markers
masking tape
mixing bowls
muffin liners
muffin tin

newspaper
newsprint
nutmeg
oatmeal
oil of cloves
oil of wintergreen
old magazines
old catalogs
paper cups
paper plates
paper punch
paper towels
pasta (uncooked)
peanut butter
pencils
pencil sharpener
pie tins
plaster of paris
plastic lids
plastic utensil
powdered drink
    mix
powdered milk
powdered sugar
powdered tempera
    paint
rice (uncooked)
rolled oats
rubbing alcohol
salt
salt shaker
sand
saucepan
scissors
sequins
sponges
spoons
spray bottles

squeeze bottles
straws (plastic)
string
sugar
sugar-free
    powdered gelatin
tacky glue
tape
tin cans
tissue paper
toilet paper tubes
tongue depressors
twigs
vanilla
vegetable oil
wallpaper paste
wallpaper samples
waxed paper
wheat flour
white glue
wood (scraps)
yarn
yogurt (plain)

special Tips and Ideas
for presenting art experiences to young children

✎ **ALWAYS supervise art experiences.** Even nontoxic art materials can cause problems. Do not let children taste anything unless you know for sure that it is safe!

✎ **ALWAYS** sit with your children and enjoy the experience with them.

✎ Art is a time for exploring and discovery. Do not be surprised if your little ones decide to use the art materials in ways that you did not consider.

✎ Spray a cooking spray on the inside of the glue lid tips. This will help to prevent clogging.

✎ Inexpensive vinyl table cloths are good to keep on hand for messy projects.

✎ Before children can learn to print, they need to develop their fine motor skills and increase their eye-hand coordination. Lacing cards and stringing beads are specific activities designed to promote this development.

✎ Put tape on the bottoms of new crayon boxes so that the bottoms will not fall out.

✎ An old shower curtain on the floor or table is great for catching spills.

✎ Add a few drops of liquid soap to any tempera paint. This will make clean up easier.

✎ Cover an entire table with butcher paper and let your little ones enjoy coloring over the whole table top!

✎ Record a favorite story, or play a commercially recorded story, while the children are "creating art."

✎ Play classical music when your children are busy creating. Research indicates that children who are exposed to classical music have a better chance of obtaining higher math and science scores when they reach school.

✎ Save yogurt cups to serve as disposable paint containers.

✎ Proudly display the creative work of your children. On pages 63 and 64 are reproducible display frames. You can mount the pictures and tape them to a refrigerator, bulletin board, wall or door.

✎ Children can create their own private art galleries with self-stick cork squares, found at many home improvement stores. The squares can be placed on any wall or surface. The children will be able to arrange and rearrange their artwork in these cork squares.

✎ Home improvement stores or paint stores now carry "chalkboard paint." Chalkboard paint can be applied to any wall, at the appropriate height for a child, and creates a surface that is easily washed. How much fun to get to write on the wall and not be in trouble!

✎ Children love to paint. Here are some interesting alternative items that can be used as paintbrushes:

- ❖ bark
- ❖ brushes
- ❖ combs
- ❖ cotton balls
- ❖ cotton swabs
- ❖ eyedroppers
- ❖ feathers

- ❖ shoe polish applicators
- ❖ spray bottles
- ❖ spoons and forks
- ❖ squeeze bottles
- ❖ string
- ❖ pipe cleaners

- ❖ fly swatters
- ❖ food
- ❖ ice
- ❖ marbles
- ❖ pipe cleaners
- ❖ roll-on deodorant bottles

✎ **ALWAYS REMEMBER:** With young children, the importance of the art experience is in the process, not in the final product.

metric conversions

If you prefer metric measurements, the art recipes in this book can easily be created by making a few simple conversions:

1/4 teaspoon = 1.25 ml
1/2 teaspoon = 2.5 ml
1 teaspoon = 5 ml
1 tablespoon = 15 ml
1 fluid ounce = 30 ml
9" x 13" baking pan = 23 cm x 32 cm baking tin

1/4 cup = 60 ml
1/3 cup = 80 ml
1/2 cup = 120 ml
2/3 cup = 160 ml
3/4 cup = 180 ml

1 cup = 240 ml
2 cups = 475 ml
1/2 inch = 1.25 cm
1 inch = 2.5 cm

1 foot = 30.48 cm
350°F = 150°C
400°F = 200°C

Super Easy Finger Paints

Think back to your childhood memories of finger painting. Most adults have fond recollections of the experience. Feeling the texture and watching the movement of the paint on the paper is a tremendous sensory experience for a small child. Here are some easy-to-make finger paint recipes that will provide you and your eager little artist with hours of fun!

Recipe One

You will need: liquid starch
powdered tempera paint
large mixing bowl
spoon or other utensil for stirring
finger paint paper

What You Do: Simply add the powdered tempera paint to the liquid starch until you have achieved the desired color. That's it! You are ready to paint!

Recipe Two

You will need: 1/2 cup boiling water
2 tablespoons dry starch
6 tablespoons cold water
food coloring
pan
spoon or other utensil for stirring
finger paint paper

What You Do: Dissolve the starch in the cold water. Add this mixture to the boiling water, stirring constantly. Heat the mixture until it becomes glossy. Add the food coloring and stir well. Let it cool completely before the children use it.

extra tips

TIP 1: For an easier cleanup, add a small amount of liquid dish washing detergent to the finger paint. Although the cleanup is easier, make sure the children still wear a paint smock or one of dad's old shirts!

TIP 2: Always make sure that you are finger painting on the shiny side of the paper.

Always supervise young children when using paint!

"Smelly" Finger Paints

Finger painting is more than a tactile experience; it can also be a multi-sensory experience. The child is feeling the paint, seeing the paint, and with this mixture, smelling the paint. These finger paints may smell good enough to eat, but don't let the children snack on their art work!

Thick Minty Finger Paint

you will need: wallpaper paste or wheat paste
water
food coloring
oil of wintergreen
large mixing bowl
spoon or other utensil for stirring
finger paint paper

what you do: Mix the wallpaper paste or wheat paste with water until you have a thin paste. Add the food coloring and a few drops of oil of wintergreen. For more fun, try adding other scents, such as vanilla, peppermint, lemon, or almond.

Clove-scented Finger Paint

you will need: 1 cup sugar
2 cups flour
2 cups cold water
6 cups boiling water
1 tablespoon boric acid
oil of cloves

food coloring
pan
large mixing bowl
spoon or other utensil for stirring
finger paint paper

what you do: Mix the flour and cold water together. Add the sugar and stir until smooth. Add the flour, cold water and sugar mixture to the 6 cups of boiling water, stirring constantly until thick. Remove from the heat and add 1 tablespoon of boric acid and several drops of the oil of cloves. Stir in the food coloring and then store the paint in sealed containers.

extra tips

Tip 1: You can also use brushes or sponges with finger paint.

Tip 2: Spread the finger paint all over the paper and practice printing letters, numbers, or drawing pictures.

"Texture" Finger Paints

Provide experiences that let your child experiment with different textures. Some children think these "funny" textures are really interesting; others will not like the strange sensation of something that feels rough. Remember to be sensitive to the reaction of your child. The following "gritty" experience can either be a lot of fun or an activity that you will not repeat!

gritty finger paint

you will need: 1 cup flour
1 cup water
food coloring
1 to 1-1/2 cups of
 salt or sand
large mixing bowl
spoon or another
 utensil for stirring
finger paint paper

what you do: Combine the flour and salt or sand. Add the water and stir until thoroughly mixed. Add the food coloring one drop at a time until you achieve the desired color.

silky smooth finger paint

you will need: 1/4 cup salt
2 tablespoons cornstarch
1 cup water
pan
spoon or other utensil for stirring
finger paint paper

what you do: Mix the water, salt, and cornstarch in a pan and bring it to a boil. Keep stirring until the mixture is the consistency of yogurt. If you want to make a variety of colors, divide the mixture and place it in different containers and add the food coloring. When cool, this mixture will feel smooth and silky.

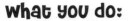

extra tip

Tip 1: The paint will last several weeks if it is put in tightly sealed containers or plastic bags and put in a refrigerator.

"edible" finger paints

Many young children have not outgrown the temptation to put everything into their mouths. Here are some fun finger paint recipes that can actually be tasted. Although these recipes are titled "edible," encourage your child to just taste the paint and not to eat the entire artistic creation!

wonderful whipped cream creations

you will need: Coolwhip™ whipped cream
food coloring
large mixing bowl
spoon or another
    utensil for stirring
thick paper or paper plate

what you do: Combine only a drop or two of food coloring with the whipped cream. Too much food coloring can make the whipped cream runny—and it is not good for children to consume too much food coloring. Just a taste, please!

super sticky finger paint

you will need: corn syrup
food coloring
various containers for storing paint
mixing bowls
spoon or other utensil for stirring
finger paint paper

what you do: Mix the corn syrup with only a drop or two of food coloring. Mix well, and then store in air-tight containers or zip-sealed plastic bags. You can create a variety of colors and store for future use. This finger paint is very sticky when wet, but when it dries, it will no longer feel sticky and will look incredibly shiny.

extra tip

TIP 1: WARNING!
Anytime a flavored gelatin is used, it will stain fingertips (which will eventually come clean) and can stain clothes and laminated counters. Be careful— but have fun!

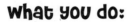

more "edible" finger paints

The following finger paint recipes are all "edible." This does not mean that the child can consume the entire art experience. Edible recipes are meant just to be tasted! Also, remind the children to wash their hands before they create any edible art experience.

instant pudding finger paint

you will need: any flavor of instant pudding
food coloring
   (only if vanilla pudding is used)
milk
large mixing bowl
spoon or other utensil for stirring
finger paint paper

what you do: Mix the pudding according to the directions on the box. Let the child use the pudding to finger paint on a paper plate. This is truly yummy art!

yummy yogurt finger paint

you will need: 1/2 carton plain yogurt
1/2 package flavored gelatin
mixing bowl
spoon or other utensil for stirring
finger paint paper

what you do: Mix all of the ingredients together and finger paint on a paper plate or on wax paper. A "healthy-to-taste" art experience!

giggly jiggly gelatin finger paint

you will need: flavored gelatin
9" x 13" pan
mixing bowl
spoon or other utensil for stirring
finger paint paper

what you do: Mix the gelatin according to the package directions. Place the gelatin in the refrigerator until it is a "gooey" consistency! Now use the gelatin to finger paint. Icky–sticky hilarious fun!

soapy paints

Your creative little artists can make huge messes. Here are some wonderful ideas for painting with an "easy-to-clean-up" ingredient—soap! The paint may be very colorful, but the tables and messy little fingers will wash up easily.

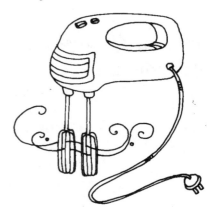

soapy flakes paint

you will need: Ivory Snow Flakes ™ detergent
water
food coloring or tempera paint
large mixing bowl
electric mixer
spoon or other utensil for stirring
thick paper or paper plate

what you do: Using an electric mixture, beat the Ivory Snow Flakes™ and water until a creamy mixture is formed. Keep the soap flakes white and finger paint on a dark-colored piece of paper. Use this paint while freshly whipped. Then try adding color to the mixture and keep on painting.

wonderful window finger paint

you will need: liquid tempera paint
paintbrushes
tape
newspapers
containers for the paint
liquid dishwashing detergent

what you do: Use the tape and newspaper to protect the walls and flooring. Mix liquid dish washing soap into the paint to help make the paint-removal easier. Let the children create a window masterpiece.

extra tips

TIP 1: WARNING! The longer the window paint is left on a window, the harder it will be to remove.

TIP 2: Cover the window with cellophane. Paint on the cellophane instead of on the window.

"no mess" painting

How much fun to paint without any mess! Here are two great ideas that allow the child the experience of painting mess-free! You will want to repeat them time and time again!

water painting

you will need: water
paintbrushes
bowls or pails

what you do: Fill bowls or pails with water. Give the each child a large paintbrush, then take the children outside and let them "water" paint the sidewalk or driveway. The children will see where they have "painted," and you will not have any mess to cleanup—although you may have some wet clothes!

no mess paint in a bag

you will need: 3 parts water
food coloring
1 part cornstarch
1 tablespoon glycerin
"zipper" freezer bag

what you do: This is a wonderful experience for little fingers to explore colors without any mess. Combine 3 parts water, 1 part cornstarch, 1 tablespoon glycerin, and a few drops of food coloring in the freezer bag. Let your child enjoy "squishing" the paint and watching the color movement in the bag. This activity is also effective for increasing fine motor strength.

extra tip

TIP 1: When water painting, have your child wear a raincoat to stay as dry as possible. If the weather is warm, wear a swimsuit.

TIP 2: When experimenting with "no mess paint in a bag," try mixing the drops of food coloring so the child can see how mixing multiple colors can create new colors. For example: red and yellow food coloring drops, mixed together, create the color orange.

Painting with "Fingers & Toes"

Capture the memory of those tiny hands and feet forever! These two art experiences can make wonderful gifts for parents or grandparents to treasure forever, and the children will think that the sensation of touching the paint is great fun.

handprints

you will need: tempera paint
paintbrushes
frame pattern on page 17
yarn
paper punch

what you do: Paint the palm of the child's hand, making sure that the entire surface is covered to the fingertips. Lay the hand down on the paper and press gently. Lift swiftly to ensure a "clean" handprint.

footprints

you will need: tempera paint
paintbrushes
frame pattern on page 17
yarn
paper punch
butcher paper

what you do: Paint the child's foot in the same manner as the handprint directions. Another fun idea is to lay a large sheet of paper on the floor and let the child walk all over it.

Punch a hole in the top of the paper, string with yarn, and hang on a wall.

extra tip

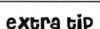

TIP 1: Hand and footprints can make adorable wrapping paper for grandparents and other family members.

TIP 2: A single handprint or footprint would also make a nice image for the front of a greeting card.

TIP 3: Frame the handprint and/or footprint and hang on a wall or display on a shelf.

Place poem here.

Handprint poem

Tiny little fingerprints on windows and walls.
Are just a reminder of when you were small.
I'll blink my eyes and you'll be grown.
I'll hold your hand in my heart – my baby – my own!

Footprint poem

Directions: Reproduce the frame pattern onto card stock. Print your child's hand or footprint using the art recipes found on page 16. Cut out and paste the poem of your choice. Punch a hole where indicated and tie with yarn for hanging.

The day you were born I counted your toes.
You were so perfect — I told everyone so.
You giggled and laughed and made my heart smile.
I am so proud that you are my child!

Spray Bottle Painting

How much fun to be able to paint while standing up, or running around! This active art experience uses spray bottles to provide your little ones with great artistic excitement. *(Be sure to have the children aim the paint at the paper or the snow.)*

Tree Easels

You will need: liquid tempera paint
spray bottles
butcher paper
tape

What You do: Tape a large piece of paper on a tree. Fill a spray bottle with diluted liquid tempera paint. Let the child stand in front of the tree and spray the paint on the paper. It's even better when you've prepared several different colors of paint to spray. Fun to create and beautiful to look at, your child's painting may look like a real Jackson Pollock work of art!

Snow Painting

You will need: water
food coloring
spray bottles

What You do: If you are lucky enough to live where there is cold weather and snow, this art experience is a must! Fill several spray bottles with water and add a little food coloring to each. Build a snowman, or whatever snow creation the child chooses to build, and spray him with color! The colored water will actually freeze and cover the snow creation with a shiny colorful ice coating.

---

extra tip

Tip 1: Bring paintbrushes outside and let the children paint facial features on the snowman.

super shiny paint

The following recipes are incredibly easy to make and will provide young children with the experience of using a paint that is shiny when dry. The children will also enjoy the smooth feel of the paint.

easy shiny paint

you will need: liquid tempera paint
white glue
paper cups
paintbrushes
paper
spoon or another
utensil for stirring
liquid dish washing detergent

what you do: Pour white glue into several paper cups. Add liquid tempera paint to each cup and stir until you reach the desired color. Dip a paintbrush in and brush the paint on the paper. As the paint dries it will not lose its shine. This paint can also be used on wood, paper, and rocks.

glossy milk paint

you will need: powdered milk
water
large mixing bowls
powdered tempera paint
paper

what you do: Mix equal parts of water and powdered milk. Add the tempera paint for color and stir. This simple paint recipe creates a paint that dries quickly and gives an opaque appearance.

---

extra tip

Tip 1: Use a cotton swab as a paintbrush with the "easy shiny paint."

Tip 2: The technique of sponge painting works well with the "glossy milk paint" recipe.

Body Painting for Kids

These are safe recipes that encourage silly fun. The first recipe creates a soapy body paint. It is highly recommended that you save this art experience for a warm summer day, when the children can wash off the paint as they run through the sprinkler. Although any shampoo or lotion will work, please use baby products for the following recipes. Baby shampoos and baby lotions have been tested and are known to be gentle for a child's skin.

Body Paint for Kids

You Will need: baby shampoo
powdered tempera paint
mixing bowls
spoon or another utensil for stirring

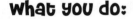

What you do: Gradually add the powdered tempera paint directly to the shampoo until you achieve the desired color and consistency. The children will giggle and giggle as they lather their bodies with color. *(Remember to have the children run through the sprinkler to wash off all of the paint.)*

Clown Face Paint

You Will need: baby lotion
powdered tempera paint
liquid dish washing detergent
mixing bowls
spoon or other utensil for stirring

What you do: Mix together 1/2 teaspoon of powdered tempera paint with 1/4 cup of baby lotion. Add a generous squirt of liquid dish washing detergent. Make a variety of clown colors. Let the children experiment with putting the clown paint on their faces. This face paint will clean up easily with soap and water.

extra tip

TIP 1: Both of these recipes are safe, but they can cause eye-irritation. Remember, any and all art experiences with young children should be supervised!

Rolling Paint

Action painting! Eager little ones will love the noise, movement, and visual appeal of this painting. Have a sink of soapy water ready for cleaning the marbles, cars, and whatever else your child decides to experiment with during the painting.

Painting with marbles

you will need: 9" x 13" cake pan
marbles
paper
liquid tempera paint
mixing bowls or paper cups
   for the paint
plastic spoons

what you do: Line the cake pan with paper. With the spoon, drop several small amounts of paint on the paper. Put in four to six marbles in the pan and tilt it back and forth. As the marbles roll around the pan, they will spread the paint in all sorts of directions, and create interesting designs.

Painting with Little Cars

you will need: 9" x 13" cake pan
toy cars and trucks
liquid tempera paint
long roll of butcher paper
pie pans for holding paint
paper towels

what you do: Pour enough paint into the pie pans so that it covers just the bottom of the pan. Roll the paper out on the floor as long as possible. Show the children how to "drive" their cars in the paint. Now, the fun part—drive the cars on the paper creating all sorts of creative tire tracks.

extra tip

TiP 1: Try rolling a variety of objects in the paint, such as golf balls, ping-pong balls, grapes, or even frozen peas.

TiP 2: On the paper, the parent or teacher can draw a road and let the child try to drive the car on the road. This is an effective pre-handwriting experience.

sponge and puffy paint

Both of these recipes provide the children with a means of exploring interesting colors, shapes, and textures. One paint allows the children to "see" the patterns and textures as they stamp the sponge around the paper. The other paint allows the children to "feel" the three-dimensional texture of the paint when it is dry.

sponge painting

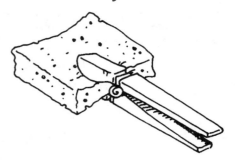

you will need: sponges, cut into small squares
pie pan
liquid tempera paint
paper
clothespins

what you do: Fill the pie pans with a variety of paint colors. Attach a clothespin to each sponge. The clothespin serves as a handle for the sponge and makes it easier for the child to manipulate it. Make one clothespin and sponge for each pan of paint, although, by the end of the experience, all the sponges will have a mixture of the paint colors. Let the children dab paint on the paper. Point out how mixing two colors can create a new color.

puffy paint

you will need: flour
salt
liquid tempera paint
card stock or cardboard
empty squeeze bottles
  (with narrow nozzles)
mixing bowls
paper towels

what you do: Mix equal parts of flour, salt, and water together in a bowl. Add tempera paint for color. Mix well and pour into a squeeze bottle that has a narrow nozzle. Squeeze the puffy paint onto cardboard or a heavy stock paper. The mixture will become hard as it dries.

---

extra tips

TIP 1: Instead of a sponge, try using a shower scrunchy for a different texture. Look for other materials that would be fun to use with paint.

TIP 2: Cut the sponges in different shapes and use them for patterning activities.

make-your-own color crayons

Playing with color crayons is an essential part of early childhood art experiences. Color crayons can provide some memorable, meaningful, and educational opportunities. Crayons are also one of the first art mediums that allow children to explore with color. These simple coloring activities can help increase and strengthen a child's fine motor skills.

solid color crayons

you will need: old broken crayons
empty tin can
saucepan
cupcake pan
cupcake liners
rack for cooling the pan

what you do: Fill the sauce pan with 2-1/2 inches of water. Take an empty tin can and "pinch" the top to create a pouring spout. Set the can in the water. Using medium heat, bring the water to boil. Fill one-fourth of the can with broken crayons of the same color. When the crayons have melted, pour the melted crayon wax into the paper cupcake liners that have been placed in the cupcake tin. Let the wax cool completely before removing the cupcake liners. Now the children can color with their own homemade color crayons!

extra tip

TIP 1: Try layering the melted wax. Pour a small amount of the melted crayon wax in the cupcake liner. Let cool and then add another color, then another, and so on.

TIP 2: Make new colors by melting different colored crayons. For example, melt red and yellow crayons to create an orange crayon.

more make-your-own color crayons

Here are some fun art experiences that can be created with crayons, including an easy and fun crayon-soap recipe. Your little ones will want to draw and create in the tub and the color will wash away with ease.

bathtub crayon soap

you will need: Ivory Snow Flakes™
water
food coloring
electric mixer
ice cube tray
mixing bowl
plastic spoons

what you do: Combine two cups of water with a generous 1/4 cup of Ivory Snow Flakes™ and mix until stiff with an electric mixer. Spoon the soapy mixture into an ice cube tray. Add 2 to 3 drops of food coloring to each section and mix with a coffee stir stick or baby spoon. Let the soap harden. These crayons are great fun in the bathtub!

---

extra tip

TIP 1: Create and name your own colors, such as "Perky Paul's Purple, Katie's Kitty Grey, Bobby's Muddy Brown."

---

homemade rainbow crayons

you will need: old broken crayons
small muffin tin
rack for cooling the pan

what you do: Fill each muffin tin, cupcake tin, or even a candy mold with broken crayons. To make rainbow crayons, place four to five different colored broken crayon pieces in each section. Place in a 400° oven just long enough for the crayons to melt. Watch carefully—crayons melt quickly. If you leave the crayons in the oven too long, the colors will blend together. You want the crayons to become soft— not liquid. Take the pan out of the oven and place it on a cooling rack. After cooling, pop out the crayons and enjoy coloring!

crayon Rubbings and scratchings

It is amazing how many wonderful activities can be created with color crayons. One of those activities is called crayon rubbings. This is the archaeological technique of rubbing over an image to create a copy of it. A second activity is "crayon scratchings." The child's art will magically appear!

crayon Rubbings

you will need: color crayons
paper
leaves and other flat items
for rubbing

what you do: Collect a variety of leaves. Remove the paper wrap from around the crayons. The best crayons are about 2 inches in length. Lay the leaf down, place the paper over it, hold the crayon on its side, and rub the crayon over the paper. Watch the leaf appear!

crayon scratchings

you will need: color crayons
paper
black tempera paint
paintbrushes
plastic utensils

extra tip

TiP 1: Place a piece of double-stick tape on the back of the leaf to help hold it in place while you rub with the crayon.

TiP 2: Try rubbing a variety of items: letters and numbers cut from card stock, seeds, coins, anything with a texture.

what you do: Give the child a piece of white construction paper and let her scribble all over the paper! Encourage the child to press hard to create heavy color. When the crayon masterpiece is complete, paint over the entire picture with black tempera paint. When the paint is still wet, let the child scratch over the picture with a plastic utensil. Even though the utensils are plastic, this activity should still be supervised.

melted crayon

This melted crayon activity is beautiful when displayed in a sun-lit window. The children will delight in watching the colors shine through their art creations. This activity utilizes an iron and ironing board. *(All the ironing should be done by an adult.)*

stained glass

you will need: waxed paper
pencil sharpener or
    cheese grater
old crayons
iron
dish towel
paper
glue
scissors
newspaper

> ### extra tip
>
> **TIP 1:** The parent or teacher can also cut out a construction paper square to frame the melted crayon art.

what you do: This project requires help and supervision from an adult. Cover a table with newspaper and place a piece of waxed paper on the newspaper. Give the child a cheese grater or a pencil sharper. Let the child either grate or sharpen many different colored crayons on the waxed paper. As soon as the child feels there are enough shavings, place another piece of waxed paper over the shavings. Pick up both pieces of waxed paper, place them on an ironing board, cover the waxed paper with a cloth, then lightly iron over the cloth. The crayons will melt and the colors will spread out over the waxed paper. Tape to a window so the sunlight will shine through the paper.

colorful glue Art

Something as simple as glue can be used for many easy art experiences and will provide hours of creative fun! The following two activities utilize the concept of color and texture. The children will love the look of this medium, as well as the feel of the glue when it is dry.

> ## extra tips
>
> **TiP 1:** Add glitter to the colored glue for an extra fun effect and added texture.
>
> **TiP 2:** Use the colored glue to write names, letters, and numbers. Trace with fingertips.

make your own colored glue

you will need: old markers
water
mixing bowl
small bottles of white glue

what you do: Don't throw away those old markers! Place them in a bowl of water and let them soak until you see the water starting to turn color. Place the soaked markers in separate bottles of glue and let them soak overnight. By the next day you will have bottles of colored glue. The children can use the glue just like a puff paint, squeezing it and creating designs on a piece of paper. The children will have fun tracing their fingers over the smooth glue lines when the art is dry.

colorful Tissue paper gluing fun

you will need: a variety of colored tissue paper
white construction paper
paintbrushes
water
white glue
paper cups

> ## extra tip
>
> **TiP 1:** You can also use this technique on objects. Cover a clay flower pot or picture frame.

what you do: Tear the tissue paper into small shapes and set aside. Mix 2 parts glue and 1 part water in a paper cup. Paint this diluted glue onto a piece of white construction paper. Pick up the tissue paper, one piece at a time, and place the shapes all over the wet glue. Different colors of tissue paper and the various shapes will make for some interesting designs. When the paper is dry, you can brush the diluted glue over the tissue paper again to create a smooth, "varnished" finish.

sticky smelly Art

Some of the most successful art activities for a young child are those that involve multi-sensory experiences. The following two activities involve the senses of sight, touch, and smell. These activities will smell good enough to eat—but don't! Provide a tasting activity using the flavors or scents used below and you will have utilized four of the five senses.

fruity smells

you will need: white glue
paintbrushes
small paper cups
instant powdered drink mix
paper plates

what you do: Pour a small amount of white glue into several paper cups. Add some of the drink mix powder. This activity is even more fun if you have several different flavors available. The children can paint the colored "flavored" glue onto paper or a paper plate. *(Make some of the drink mix so the children can taste what they are seeing and smelling.)* Let them touch the glue when it is dry. Have them smell their fingers. Did the scent rub onto their fingertips?

spicy smells

you will need: various spices
white glue
paintbrushes
small paper cups
paper plates

what you do: Follow the directons above, but instead of using powdered drink mixes, use spices—cinnamon, onion, garlic, cloves, nutmeg, peppermint, lemon, or anything else you would like to experiment with. This is really fun and can result in lots of silly laughing.

extra tips

TiP 1: Let the children smell the scents when they are wet and when they are dry. Compare the difference.

TiP 2: When the glue is dry, play "guess the flavor."

TiP 3: Make a graph of which "smells" the children liked and which ones they did not like.

construction Art

It is great fun simply to glue things together. The children can experiment with how things fit together and how they stick to one another. This process of trial and error is wonderful for developing problem-solving skills. These activities incorporate two favorites of young children: sticky art materials, and the concept of building and stacking objects.

Buildings/sculptures on paper

You will need: white glue
cotton swabs
craft sticks
cardboard
tacky white glue
craft sticks

extra tip

TIP 1: Try using other materials for this project: colored toothpicks, small twigs, or even tongue depressors.

What you do: Pour a small amount of white glue in a paper cup. Give the child the glue, a heavy piece of paper or a piece of cardboard, cotton swabs, and many craft sticks. Have the child dip the cotton swab tip into the glue and use it to apply the glue to the craft sticks. Let the child glue the craft sticks onto the cardboard in any pattern. Five and six-year-olds might try use the craft sticks to construct the shape of a house or building.

3-D Buildings/sculptures

You will need: small wood pieces
tacky white glue
cotton swabs
small paper cups
paper plates

extra tip

TIP 1: Try adding other objects to the wood sculpture, such as buttons, beads, or pictures from magazines.

What you do: Pour a small amount of white glue into a paper cup. Give the child a variety of small pieces of wood *(balsa wood works well and is easy to manipulate)*, a paper plate, cotton swabs, and the glue. Using the paper plate as a base, the children can use the cotton swab to apply the glue to the wood pieces, stacking the wood into any shape or three-dimensional form.

shaker Art

These glue activities provide young children with textural experiences. One experience utilizes salt and the other sand. The children will enjoy feeling their art when it is dry. Think about what other items you could put in a salt shaker that children could use to shake on a glue design. *(The shaking is the fun part!)*

salt shaker Art

you will need: white glue
salt shaker filled with salt
dark paper
    (black, dark blue, or purple)
cardboard
paintbrushes
9" x 13" cake pan

what you do: Pour a small amount of diluted white glue into a paper cup. Give the glue to the child, along with a heavy piece of dark-colored construction paper, a paintbrush, and a filled salt shaker. Put the paper in a 9" x 13" cake pan. Have the child paint a design with the glue. Shake the salt over the glue. Shake off the excess salt. The salt will sparkle in the sunlight, and on the dark paper it will look like snow.

Texture Art

you will need: white glue
9" x 13" cake pan
light-blue paper
salt shaker filled with sand
paintbrushes

what you do:

Pour a small amount of diluted white glue into a paper cup. Give the glue to the child, along with a piece of light-blue construction paper, a paintbrush, and the sand. Put the paper in a 9" x 13" cake pan. Paint glue on the paper and then sprinkle the sand over the glue. Shake off the excess sand. Add small sea shells for fun.

extra tips

Tip 1: Try using chopped parsley.

Tip 2: Color white sand with food coloring. Put wet white sand in a jar, sprinkle in food coloring, and shake. Let the sand dry before putting it in a salt shaker.

Bubble Recipes

All children have great fun when they are making, blowing, and playing with bubbles. The next few pages will provide you with recipes, new ideas, homemade bubble wands, bubble art, and bubble games. Get ready to hear all the squeals of laughter when you introduce the joy of bubbles!

Recipe 1: The easiest Bubbles

You will need: 2 tablespoons
      dishwashing detergent
1 cup water
a jar to store the bubble mix

What you do: Mix together and enjoy!

Recipe 2: The greatest Bubbles

You will need: 1 cup water
2 tablespoons light corn syrup or
      2 tablespoons glycerin
4 tablespoons dishwashing detergent

What you do: Mix together and have loads of fun!

Recipe 3: Swishy Sweet Bubbles

You will need: 1 cup water
2 tablespoons light corn syrup
2 tablespoons
      dishwashing detergent

What you do: It's so sweet that you should not use it when bees and wasps are nearby.

Recipe 4: Fancy Bubbles

You will need: 1 cup water
1 tablespoon glycerin
2 tablespoons
      dishwashing detergent
1 teaspoon sugar

What you do: Stir. The mixture will be ready for blowing bubbles once the sugar dissolves.

extra tip

Special tip for Babies and Toddlers: You need to be careful when using bubbles around babies' or toddlers' eyes. Substitute baby shampoo or baby soap for the dish detergent in all the bubble recipes.

extra tips

Tip 1: For the best results with any bubble recipe, make the bubble mix the day before you plan to use it.

Tip 2: Glycerin (*found at any drug store*) can be added to most bubble recipes and will help create stronger and better bubbles.

COlOrful Bubble Recipes

These two colorful bubble recipes are messy, but a lot of fun. All of the bubbles, whether you add color or not, already have color. If you look carefully at a bubble as it floats, you can see a wide range of colors. When you add food coloring or tempera paint to the bubble mixture, the bubbles will be saturated with color!

Recipe 1: Bubble Color

you will need: 2 tablespoons dishwashing detergent
1 cup liquid tempera paint
1 tablespoon liquid starch
a jar to store the bubble mixture

what you do: Add a few drops of water if the mixture is too thick.

Recipe 2: Colorful Bubbles

you will need: 1 quart of warm water
1 cup sugar or
powdered soap detergent
food coloring
plastic straws
small juice cans

extra tip

TIP 1: For the best results, make sure that the containers used to store the bubble mixtures are very clean. Any dirt in the container can ruin your chance of blowing great bubbles!

what you do: Be sure to dissolve the soap or sugar in warm water.

make your own bubble wands

Bubbles are probably the most fun when the children have bubble wands and can wave beautiful bubbles through the air! Children love running outside and chasing all their exciting bubbles.

coat hanger wands

you will need: coat hanger
wire cutter
10"–12" piece of string

what you do: Cut out a 12" section of coat hanger. Tie a 10" to 12" loop of string on the end. Dip the loop in the bubble mixture and wave it through the air.

plastic lid wands

you will need: Plastic lids from
yogurt, butter, coffee, or cottage cheese containers
dowel rod
tacks or staple gun
scissors

what you do: Cut out the center of a plastic lid. Attach the lid to a dowel rod using a staple gun or tack. Dip the lid into the bubble mixture and wave through the air.

more Bubble wands

Here are some additional ideas for creating bubble wands. There is even an idea for blowing bubbles using only your hands! It might take some practice, but it is well worth the effort. Even small children can master this magical feat!

Fly swatters

you will need: fly swatters
bubble mixture

what you do: Fly swatters are inexpensive and can create thousands of tiny bubbles.

Plastic cookie cutters

you will need: cookie cutters
bubble mixture

what you do: Cookie cutters make great bubble wands. The size of the bubbles will depend on the size of the cookie cutter.

Plastic fruit baskets

you will need: small plastic fruit baskets
bubble mixture

what you do: Small plastic fruit baskets can make effective bubble wands. Dip the fruit basket in the bubble mixture and wave through the air.

Creating Bubbles without any wands

you will need: hands
bubble mixture

what you do: This might take some practice, but children can create huge bubbles using only their hands. Have the children lock their thumbs together and spread their fingers to create a closed circle. Have them dip their hands in the bubble mixture and blow.

Bubble Art

Bubbles are not just fun for blowing and chasing, but can be used for many other activities, too. Here are some entertaining art experiences that utilize bubbles. Get ready for some really messy fun as children learn about science, art, and how to predict what will happen when a bubble pops!

Bubble Popping Art

you will need: bubble mixture
liquid tempera paint
white construction paper
bubble wand or
    drinking straws
paper cups
newspaper

what you do: Wear a paint shirt and have a lot of newspaper on hand. Pour the bubble mixture into each of the paper cups. Add just enough liquid tempera paint to color the bubble mixture. Stir gently. Blow bubbles and try to catch them on the white paper. When the bubbles "pop" on the paper, they will leave beautiful paint splotches and patterns. This is a really exciting art experience for the children.

Bubble Sculpture

you will need: bubble mixture
paper plate
freezer

what you do: Blow a bunch of bubbles on a paper plate. Quickly, before the bubbles have time to pop, place them on a shelf in the freezer. Don't peek. Leave them there for at least three hours and then have the children look inside. They will be so surprised at what is in the freezer.

Bubble game experiences

One of the most interesting characteristics about bubbles is that you can actually play with them. Children delight in chasing them, trying to catch them, and popping them with their fingers.

hoola hoop Bubbles

you will need: bubble mixture
hoola hoop
small wading pool

what you do: This activity is designed for a warm summer day. Fill the wading pool with the bubble mixture. Dip a hoola hoop in the pool and wave in the air. An adult will probably have to do this, but it will enchant small children. Never have there been bigger bubbles for them to see!

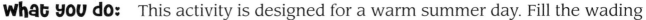

Bubble contest

you will need: bubble mixture
bubble wands or blower
friends

what you do: Have a group of children blow as many bubbles as they can. Count who has the most bubbles in the air. Who can blow the bubble that floats the highest? Who can blow the biggest bubble? Who can blow the smallest bubble?

The Longest Floater

you will need: bubble mixture
bubble wands or blower
friends

what you do: Have each of the children blow a bubble and see how long they can keep their bubble floating without popping.

"make your own" sidewalk chalk

There is something special about chalk to young children. The feel of the chalk in their hands, the way it looks on a sidewalk, driveway, or construction paper, and the way it feels as it moves across a rough texture. Children also love having the ability to create pictures on sidewalks and driveways. Your little sidewalk artists will thoroughly enjoy the chalk activities and experiences found on the following pages.

Big sidewalk chalk sticks

you will need: 2 cups plaster of paris
2 cups cold water
toilet paper cardboard tubes
plastic mixing bowl
disposable stir sticks
tempera paint
duct tape
cookie sheet
newspaper/waxed paper

extra tip

Tip 1: NEVER pour plaster of paris down your sink. Pour all excess in the garbage!

what you do: Cover the bottom of the cookie sheet with waxed paper. Duct tape one end of each toilet paper tube and set them on the cookie sheet with the taped side down. Prepare the plaster of paris in the mixing bowl. Slowly add the water and blend with a disposable stir stick. When the mixture resembles the texture of pudding, add the tempera paint.

Once the mixture is prepared, pour it into the toilet paper tubes. Gently tap the sides of the tubes to eliminate any air bubbles. Since these will be large chalk sticks, they will need two days to completely dry. After drying, tear off the cardboard tube and have the children go and create!

extra tip

Tip 1: Design your own sidewalk hopscotch game or draw some fun mazes!

more "make your own" sidewalk chalk

Here are two more recipes for sidewalk chalk. These chalk sticks also make wonderful birthday party or school party gifts!

Little Sidewalk Chalk Sticks

you will need: 1 cup plaster of paris
1/2 cup cold water
candy molds
plastic mixing bowl
disposable stir sticks
tempera paint

---

extra tip

TIP 1: AGAIN! NEVER pour plaster of paris down your sink. Pour all excess in the garbage!

---

what you do: Pour the plaster of paris into the mixing bowl. Slowly add the water and stir with a disposable stir stick. When the mixture resembles the texture of pudding, add the tempera paint. Pour the mixture into the candy molds and let it dry completely—at least four hours. Pop the chalk out of the molds and have the children create some great drawings!

Rainbow Sidewalk Chalk

you will need: 2 cups plaster of paris
2 cups cold water
toilet paper cardboard tubes
plastic mixing bowls
disposable stir sticks
tempera paint
duct tape
cookie sheet
newspaper/waxed paper

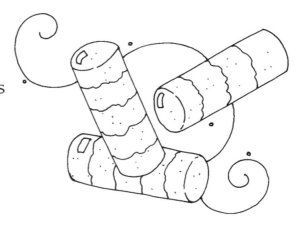

what you do: Cover the bottom of the cookie sheet with waxed paper. Duct tape one end of each toilet paper tube and set them with the tape side down on the cookie sheet. Pour the plaster of paris into the mixing bowl, then slowly add the water and stir. Pour the plaster into three or four bowls. Add a different color of tempera paint to each bowl. Layer the various colored plasters into the toilet paper tubes. Let dry and then remove the cardboard tubes.

Terrific Chalk Recipes

Here are a few more recipes that your little ones will love. The children will delight in being able to help prepare, and then use, these new chalks.

Incredible Eggshell Chalk

You will need: 6 to 8 washed eggshells
1 teaspoon hot water
1 teaspoon flour
food coloring or tempera paint

---

extra tip

Tip 1: Tape a large piece of paper to a tree or cover the sidewalk with paper!

What you do: Wash the eggshells and dry well. They should be free of any egg residue. Take them outside, or somewhere that you don't mind a mess, and grind the shells into a powder. *(You may also grind them in a blender.)* Remove any large shell pieces from the powder. In a small dish, mix the flour and eggshell powder with very hot water until it looks like a thick paste. You can add a drop or two of food coloring or tempera paint for color.

Roll the mixture into the shape of chalk sticks and wrap them in paper towels or cloths. The incredible eggshell chalk will need approximately three days to dry.

Silly Spray Chalk

You will need: 4 tablespoons cornstarch
1 cup warm water
food coloring
spray bottles

What you do: Mix the cornstarch and water in a bowl. Make sure that the cornstarch dissolves completely. Add food coloring to get the desired color. Pour into a spray bottle and shake well. This spray will look like chalk after it dries. It can be sprayed on sand, snow, sidewalks, and paper.

creative chalk Art

These two recipes, one with starch and one with buttermilk, will leave an interesting finish and will prevent the colored chalk from smudging or rubbing off.

sensational starch chalk Art

you will need: colored chalk
liquid starch
paintbrush
water
construction paper

what you do: In a bowl, mix together equal parts of water and liquid starch. Have the child brush the mixture all over a piece of construction paper. Then have the children draw on the wet paper with colored chalk. When the paper dries, the starch will act as a fixative and the chalk will not smear.

extra tip

TiP 1: Purchase some refrigerator magnets so you can display all the masterpiece art!

Buttermilk chalk Art

you will need: colored chalk
buttermilk
plastic mixing bowl
water
construction paper

what you do: Brush the buttermilk over a piece of construction paper or manilla paper *(file folders work well).* Draw with colored chalk on the paper when it is still wet from the buttermilk. When dry, the drawing will have an interesting finish.

more creative chalk art

Here are two fun ideas for creating beautiful chalk drawings that provide for both bright colors and interesting textures.

sweet water chalk art

you will need: colored chalk
plastic mixing bowl
water
sugar
construction paper

what you do: Fill a bowl with water and add several tablespoons of sugar. Place the colored chalk in the water and let it soak for no more than five minutes. Now have the children draw with the wet chalk on the construction paper. When the chalk dries, it will have an interesting look. Try the same experience without the sugar in the water. Can you see a difference?

wet paint chalk art

you will need: colored chalk
plastic mixing bowl
water
white liquid tempera paint
spoon or other utensil
    to stir the paint
dark-colored construction paper
    (black, dark blue, or purple)

what you do:  Pour some white tempera paint into a small bowl. Have the children dip the tip of the colored chalk into the white paint and draw on the construction paper. You can see the colors of the chalk through the paint, and the white edges created by the paint provide an interesting finish. Experiment with different colors of paint.

"make your own" cooked playdough

Playdough is an absolute necessity, and should be a staple item on every early childhood equipment list. It fosters creativity, imagination, stimulates sensory awareness, and strengthens fine motor skills. The following pages are filled with "easy-to-make" and creative playdough ideas!

The Best Basic Playdough

you will need:

(LARGE BATCH)	(SMALL BATCH)
3 cups flour	1 cup flour
1-1/2 cups salt	1/2 cup salt
3 tablespoons cream of tartar	1 tablespoon cream of tartar
3 cups water	1 cup water
3 tablespoons vegetable oil	3/4 tablespoon vegetable oil
food coloring	food coloring

what you do: Add the food coloring to the water. Mix the flour, salt, cream of tartar, vegetable oil, water, and food coloring together in a saucepan. Cook over a low heat, stirring constantly, until the dough is no longer sticky. Cool the dough and place into a plastic bag that seals tightly. Knead the dough in the plastic bag for several minutes, and then store in the refrigerator.

 extra tips

TiP 1: For even distribution of color, add the food coloring to the water before the water is mixed with the other ingredients.

TiP 2: Remember to store the playdough in airtight containers and refrigerate. This will help the playdough last for several weeks.

"make your own" terrific playdough

These are two of the easiest and most popular playdough recipes!

no-cook baker's clay

you will need: 4 cups flour
1 cup salt
1 teaspoon powered alum
2 cups water
food coloring

extra tip

TIP 1: Turn common household objects into tools to be used while playing with playdough: cookie cutters, plastic silverware, garlic press, rolling pins, melon baller, ice cream scoop.

what you do: Mix the flour, salt, and powdered alum together. Slowly mix the water into the flour mixture, and then knead for several minutes. Divide the dough into smaller balls and then add a different food coloring to each section of dough. Store in airtight containers.

This dough can be baked. Use cookie cutters or create your own shapes. Place on an ungreased cookie sheet and bake for 30 minutes in an oven set at 250°. Turn the dough over and bake another 30 minutes.

great play clay

you will need: 1 cup cornstarch
2 cups baking soda
1-1/4 cups water
liquid tempera paint
  or food coloring
mixing bowl
microwave-safe bowl

extra tip

special tip: Add vanilla extract to any homemade playdough recipe and it will help prevent mold, preserve the dough, and smell great!

what you do: Mix the cornstarch and baking soda together in a mixing bowl. In a microwave-safe bowl, mix the water with the paint or food coloring. Slowly add the flour mixture to the water and stir. Microwave the mixture for several minutes, stopping to stir every 30 to 40 seconds, or cook on the stove over a low heat for approximately 15 to 20 minutes while stirring constantly. This playdough will harden if air-dried and may be painted.

"make your own" sand playdough

Playdough made with sand has the effect of combining the texture of the sand and the smoothness of playdough into one great fine motor experience. The following recipes are unusual and are guaranteed to delight your little ones.

no-cook super sand playdough

you will need: 4 cups of clean play sand
3 cups flour
1 cup water
1/4 cup vegetable oil

extra tip

Tip 1: Clear nail polish can be used as a varnish.

what you do: Combine the flour, salt, water, and oil in a mixing bowl. Knead with your hands until the mixture forms a ball. If the mixture is too dry, gradually add water until it reaches a nice dough consistency. If the mixture is too watery, gradually add more flour. This is a super playdough for children who really enjoy tactile experiences.

sensational sand castle clay

you will need: 2 cups sand
1 cup water
1 cup cornstarch
mixing bowl
saucepan
spoon or utensil for stirring

what you do: Mix the ingredients in a saucepan and cook over a low heat until thick and clay-like. Let the children mold their vision of a sand castle or sand fort!

"make your own" snow playdough

It doesn't matter whether it is summer or winter, or warm or cold outside, children will have fun playing with snow playdough. Here are two very different recipes—one actually looks like snow, the other makes use of small white cotton balls. If you call the playdough "snowdough," many young children will spontaneously try to mold snowmen!

Fluffy snow playdough

you will need: 1 cup Ivory Snow Flakes™ detergent
3 cups warm water
mixing bowl
electric mixer

What you do: First add the food coloring to the water. Then add the soap flakes and beat with an electric mixer until the soap is fluffy and can be manipulated. If you want to pretend that this is "real" snow, leave out the food coloring and simply make "snow white" playdough.

cotton snowball dough fun

you will need: 1 cup flour
1 cup water
mixing bowl
spoon or utensil for stirring
cotton balls

What you do: Mix the flour and water together to form a paste. If the paste mixture is too watery, gradually add a little more flour. Add small amounts of water if the paste is too stiff. Dip the cotton balls into the paste mixture and mold a sculpture. Bake the sculpture for an hour at 325° until it becomes light brown in color. After the sculpture is cool, it can be painted.

special playdough Recipes

Here are two extra fun ideas for creating with playdough.

sparkly playdough

you will need: 1 cup flour
1 cup water
1/2 cup salt
1 tablespoon vegetable oil
2 teaspoons cream of tartar
food coloring
saucepan
spoon or utensil for stirring
glitter

what you do: Mix all the ingredients together in a saucepan over a medium-low heat. Keep stirring until the dough forms a ball. Remove the dough from the pan and cool. Add glitter to the dough and knead until smooth. This is one playdough recipe that should NOT be refrigerated. Stored in an air-tight container, this playdough will last for several weeks at room temperature.

playdough handprints

you will need: 1 cup flour   food coloring
1/2 cup salt   saucepan
1 cup water
1 tablespoon cream of tartar
2 tablespoons vegetable oil
spoon or utensil for stirring

 extra tip

TiP 1: Poke a hole in the playdough with a plastic straw so the playdough creation can be hung for display.

what you do: Mix the water, vegetable oil, and food coloring in a saucepan. Bring the liquid mixture almost to a boil. Remove the pan from the heat and add the dry ingredients. Mix well. When the dough is cool, knead for several minutes.

Roll the dough into a ball and press into a circle or oval about an inch thick. Have the child press her hand into the clay so that it leaves a nice hand impression. Bake at 200° for approximately one-half hour or until the dough hardens. The baking time may vary depending on the size and thickness of the dough.

Playdough Recipes made with natural food

The following are two unique playdough recipes. One smells great and the other is great fun to touch!

natural playdough

you will need: 1 cup flour
1 cup water
1/2 cup salt
1 tablespoon vegetable oil
2 tablespoons cream of tartar
mixing bowl/saucepan
spoon or utensil for stirring
fruit and vegetable juices

what you do: Mix the flour, salt, and oil together in a saucepan, and then slowly add the water. Cook over a medium heat while stirring constantly. The dough will be ready when it forms a ball and becomes stiff. Divide the dough into three or four different balls. Add one of the following vegetable or fruit juices to each ball of dough for coloring: grape juice, carrot juice, beet juice, spinach juice, or orange juice. The juices will provide the color for the playdough as well as adding a wonderful aroma to the dough.

cornmeal playdough

you will need: 1-1/2 cups flour
1-1/2 cups cornmeal
1 cup salt
1 cup water
food coloring
mixing bowl
spoon or utensil for stirring

what you do: Mix the flour and cornmeal in a mixing bowl. Add the food coloring to the water and then mix into the flour. Knead the dough until it is easy to manipulate. This playdough has an interesting texture and is fun to squish!

super sweet
playdough Recipes

These playdough recipes smell so good that the children will want to gobble them up! The chocolate recipe can be tasted *(just a small nibble)*, but the juicy fruit dough should not be eaten. Both of these playdough recipes will make for great art experiences.

Juicy Fruit playdough

you will need: 2 cups flour
1 cup salt
1 cup boiling water
2 tablespoons vegetable oil
4 tablespoons cream of tartar
3 ounce package of
    sugar-free gelatin
saucepan
spoon or utensil for stirring

 extra tip

Tip 1: Use a pastry board when working with home-made playdough. There will not be as much sticking.

what you do: Mix all of the ingredients together in a mixing bowl. Bring the water and oil to a boil and then pour in the other ingredients. Turn the heat to low and stir the ingredients until the mixture forms a ball. Pour onto a piece of waxed paper to cool. Once the playdough is cool, enjoy the great-smelling playdough fun!

Chewy Chocolate playdough

you will need: 10 ounces of semi-sweet chocolate
1/3 cup light corn syrup
mixing bowl
spoon or utensil for stirring

what you do: Chop the chocolate into small pieces. Place the chocolate in a double-boiler and melt. Pour the corn syrup into the melted chocolate and stir. Pour the mixture onto waxed paper and spread it around evenly, then cover the mixture with another sheet of waxed paper. The chocolate will begin to thicken within a couple of hours. It is best to let the chocolate sit overnight. The next day, it will be pliable and can be molded just like real play-dough.

Cinnamon Spicy Playdough Recipes

These playdough recipes might remind you of a holiday or of the wonderful smells that came from grandmother's kitchen. Enjoy the aroma as the children create!

Spicy Playdough

You will need: 3 tablespoons nutmeg
2 tablespoons ground cloves
3/4 cup cinnamon
1 cup applesauce
mixing bowl
spoon or utensil for stirring
rolling pin

What you do: Mix all of the ingredients together in a mixing bowl. Let the children have the fun of adding all the ingredients and stirring. Use a rolling pin to flatten out the dough, just like one would roll out cookie dough. Have the children cut out different shapes with cookie cutters. Poke a hole in the top of each shape so they can be hung. Place all the shapes on waxed paper, cover them with another sheet of waxed paper, and let dry for several days. Be sure to turn the shapes so they dry evenly.

Cinnamon Playdough

You will need: 1 cup salt
2 cups whole wheat flour
5 teaspoons cinnamon
2 tablespoons vegetable oil
1 cup warm water
food coloring
2 mixing bowls
spoon or utensil for stirring

What you do: Combine all of the dry ingredients together in a mixing bowl. In another bowl, mix together the food coloring, water, and vegetable oil. Add the flour mixture gradually to the water until you reach the desired consistency. Stir until it forms a ball. Knead the dough and have fun playing!

oatmeal Playdough Recipes

Oatmeal can add an interesting texture to playdough. There is no cooking involved so these are very easy recipes to make. They are also great recipes for little helpers to make!

uncooked oatmeal Playdough

you will need: 1 cup flour
2 cups oatmeal
1 cup water
mixing bowl
spoon or utensil for stirring

extra tip

TiP 1: Adding cornmeal or ground coffee into the playdough can provide other interesting textures.

what you do: Combine the flour and oatmeal in a mixing bowl. While stirring, gradually add the water. Knead the stiff dough until it is smooth and pliable. Do you like the way it smells? How does it feel?

tasteable oatmeal Playdough

you will need: 2 cups creamy peanut butter
2 cups rolled oats or oatmeal
2 cups powdered milk
2/3 cup honey
food coloring
mixing bowl
spoon or utensil for stirring

what you do: Mix all the ingredients together in a large bowl. Stir and knead until it feels like playdough. This dough is great fun to play with. It is "tasteable," but it is recommended only in very small samples.

 extra tip

TiP 1: For older children, add other fun foods to the tasteable oatmeal playdough: tiny chocolate chips, various cereals, or tiny hard candies.

Playdough

Candy and Coffee Playdough Recipes

Candy and coffee sound like funny ingredients for playdough. The yummy candy playdough recipe can be tasted and smells great. The coffee playdough is incredibly smooth. Children seem to either really like or dislike this smell. Teachers and parents might enjoy playing with *(and smelling)* this playdough!

Yummy Candy Playdough

You will need: 1/3 cup margarine
1/3 cup light corn syrup
16 ounces of powdered sugar
1 teaspoon vanilla
food coloring
mixing bowl
spoon or utensil for stirring

What you do: Mix together the margarine, light corn syrup, vanilla, and food coloring. Gradually stir in the powdered sugar. Knead until smooth. Have fun molding with this playdough and it's alright to have a taste!

Cool Coffee Playdough

You will need: 4 cups flour
1 cup salt
1/4 cup instant coffee
1-1/2 cups warm water
2 mixing bowls
spoon or utensil for stirring

What you do: Dissolve the instant coffee in the warm water and set aside. In another bowl mix the flour and salt. Using a spoon, make a hole in the center of the flour-and-salt mixture. Pour the coffee in the hole, stir with a spoon, and then knead with your hands. This playdough should be very smooth. This playdough can also be hardened by baking. Place the shapes the child has made on a cookie sheet and bake in an oven at 300° for an hour.

Pliable Peanut Butter Playdough Recipes

You might be surprised to discover that peanut butter is one of the best ingredients to use when creating a homemade playdough recipe. The smell and texture of creamy peanut butter will delight young children as they play, squish, and create with these "yummy" recipes!

Easy Edible Peanut Butter Playdough

You will need:
- 1 cup creamy peanut butter
- 1 cup light corn syrup
- 1 cup powdered sugar
- 3 cups powdered milk
- mixing bowl
- spoon or utensil for stirring

What you do: Mix together the peanut butter, corn syrup, and powdered sugar. Gradually stir in the powdered milk. Knead all the ingredients together until you have a smooth dough. Smooth, yummy fun!

Fun-to-Touch Peanut Butter Playdough

You will need:
- 1 cup creamy peanut butter
- 1 cup honey
- 1 cup powdered milk
- 1 cup rolled oats
- 1 mixing bowl
- spoon or utensil for stirring

What you do: Put all the ingredients in a bowl and mix. This peanut butter playdough recipe is grainier to the touch than the "Easy Edible Peanut Butter Playdough."

 extra tip

TIP 1: For extra fun, or for making funny faces on the peanut butter playdough sculptures, add: raisins, butterscotch and chocolate chips, hard candies, dried fruit, nuts, and pretzels.

coloring Rice and pasta noodles

Colored rice and pasta can be wonderful materials for use in a multitude of art experiences. For example, the colored rice can be used for mosaics by spreading glue on paper and letting the children drop the rice onto the paper. In addition, colored pasta can provide hours of beading and jewelry-making fun.

Rice and pasta noodles

You will need: a variety of uncooked
pasta noodles or rice
2 teaspoons food coloring
3 teaspoons rubbing alcohol
container with an air-tight lid
waxed paper

What you do: Mix the food coloring and the rubbing alcohol in the container. Place the pasta or rice in the container and cover. Then shake the container so the color is evenly distributed on the rice and pasta. Spread the colored rice or pasta onto waxed paper and allow to dry. It will take several hours for the pasta to dry completely.

The colored rice or pasta can be used for many different art experiences. Both can be glued on paper, pots, or wood. The pasta noodles can also be used for stringing and patterning activities.

extra tip

TIP 1: Instead of a plastic tub container, a plastic bag that seals can be used for coloring the rice or pasta.

extra tips

TIP 2: Color many varieties of pasta noodles and place in a bucket with string or yarn. Colored pasta noodles are excellent for beading and patterning activities.

TIP 3: Wrap masking tape around the yarn to serve as a needle when stringing pasta noodles.

"goopy Stuff" Recipes

These are two "goopy" recipes that children will love to touch and feel. The sensation of molding, stretching, smooshing, and swishing the goopy stuff is so much fun! Even as an adult you might find yourself wanting to play with "the goop."

Rubbery goop

you will need: 2 cups baking soda
1-1/2 cups water
1 cup cornstarch

what you do: Place all the ingredients in a saucepan over medium heat and stir until smooth. This mixture needs to boil and be stirred constantly until it is thick. Remove from the heat and cool. Now let the children enjoy the feel and texture, as well as the movement, of this rubbery goop!

Slimy goop

you will need: 1/2 cup white glue
food coloring *(optional)*
1/4 cup liquid starch
wooden spoon

what you do: Put all the ingredients in a bowl and mix with a wooden spoon, craft stick, or tongue depressor. Let the children get their fingers sticky and have a lot of "goopy" fun!

sparkle art

All young children seem to be attracted to things that sparkle—they are fun to look at and frequently fun to touch. Here are some ideas that can help to make many of your art experiences "sparkle."

---

extra tip

TiP 1: For convenience, make a variety of colored salt glitter and keep it on hand.

"make your own" sparkle glitter

you will need: 1/2 cup salt
7 to 8 drops of food coloring

what you do: Combine the salt and coloring in a bowl and stir until the color is evenly distributed over the salt. Set the colored salt in the sun to dry or place in the microwave for 30 to 60 seconds. When the salt is completely dry, it can be stored in a salt shaker and used just like glitter.

sparkly scribble pictures

you will need: crayons
dark construction paper
water
salt
paintbrush

what you do: Let the child scribble or color with a crayon anything he would like to draw. When the colored masterpiece is finished, provide the child with a paintbrush and a small bowl of very salty water. Have the child paint the salty water over the drawing. The crayon picture will sparkle when it dries.

sand casting Little handprints

Although young children will have fun participating in and helping with this art experience, the activity is really designed more for parents. The image of a tiny hand is one that all parents will want to remember. This can be made for parents, grandparents, or as a decoration to hang in the child's room. Enjoy this activity and remember to hold that little hand as much as you can while it is still little!

sand casting handprints

you will need: sand
spray bottle filled
with water
mixing bowl
plaster of paris
bucket

extra tip

TiP 1: Children enjoy making sand casts. Make other impressions in the sand. Rocks, buttons, marbles, and other objects can be pressed into the plaster when it is still soft and not completely dry.

what you do: Fill a bucket with damp sand. Use the spray bottle filled with water to keep the sand damp. Have the child press the palm of his or her hand into the sand, making sure that a clean impression is made. Also make sure that there is at least an inch of sand all the way around the impression.

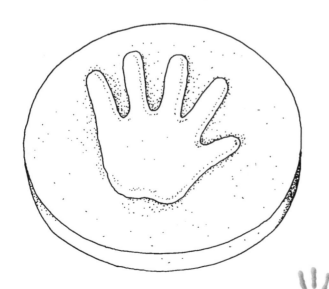

Mix the plaster of paris with water until it is the consistency of whipped cream. Pour the plaster into the impression of the hand. Make sure that the entire impression is filled. Let it dry overnight, then lift out and brush off the sand.

The child may also enjoy painting his handprint with tempera paint. An adult can spray the plaster handprint with a clear varnish.

pretty-easy printmaking

Printmaking is a fun activity for young children. It gives the children an opportunity to see cause and effect, and to learn how identical images can be created.

fancy finger paint prints

you will need: finger paint
finger paint paper
white construction paper

what you do: Tape a piece of finger paint paper on a table top. Let the child create a finger paint masterpiece. Once the painting is finished, press a piece of white construction paper on top of the finger-painting and lift off. You will now have an exact copy of the finger painting.

option: Finger paint on only one-half of the paper. While it is still wet, fold the paper over to create an exact print on the other side of the paper.

nature printing

you will need: tempera paint
pie tin
paper
various objects
  from nature:
  *(vegetables and fruit
  cut in half and leaves)*

what you do: Pour tempera paint into the pan. Pour just enough paint to cover the bottom of the pan. Lay an object, such as a leaf, in the paint, then gently press it to the paper.

creative coloring

Crayons are probably the first art materials that young children are able to use *(and are allowed to use!).* For children, there is something magical about watching the color appear. However, little hands can have a difficult time holding and manipulating crayons. Here is an idea to make it easier for your person with little hands to use crayons.

chubby chubby crayons

you will need: color crayons
paper
tape

extra tip

Tip 1: Tape several different colors together so children can experience using "rainbow crayons."

what you do: Tape several crayons together. This chubby chubby crayon is easier for a young child to hold and creates several lines at once. Read the extra tip for another fun coloring idea!

color. color. and more color

The following activities give children the opportunity to experiment with color.

paper plate magic

you will need: water-based color makers
heavy paper plates
spray bottle with water

what you do: Give the child a paper plate and let her color all over it with water-based markers. When the child has finished her drawing, give her the spray bottle and let her give her drawing a "spray." The plates will look beautiful and it's great fun to watch the colors blend together.

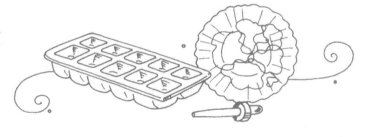

coloring coffee filters

you will need: paper
ice cube tray
eyedroppers
coffee filters

what you do: Lay flat a dry circular coffee filter. Fill the sections of an ice cube tray with water. Add several drops of food coloring to each section of the ice cube tray. Using eyedroppers, drop the colored water on the coffee filter. The more color you add, the more the colors will spread and blend.

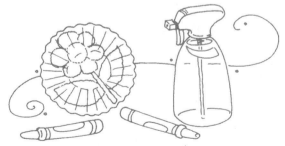

wonderful wet coffee filters

you will need: water-based color makers
coffee filters
spray bottle with water

what you do: Lay flat a coffee filter and spray with water until it is fairly wet. Using water-based markers, draw on the filter. The colors will blend and spread.

sensational scissor fun

Scissors are very difficult for a child to learn how to use properly. It takes both fine motor maturity and practice. Here are some excellent ideas to help your child gain confidence and master the skill of using a scissors.

snipping funny shapes

you will need: scissors
contact paper
construction paper

what you do: Let your child enjoy cutting colored construction paper. It does not matter how big or what shapes the pieces are. The adult should cut out and remove the backing on an 8.5" x 11" piece of contact paper. When the child has a small pile of colored shapes, she can simply "stick" the shapes on the contact paper. When finished, the contact paper can be turned over and stuck to another sheet of paper. The result is a work of scissor art ready for display.

scissor cutting magazines and catalogs

you will need: scissors
glue sticks
construction paper
old magazines and catalogs

what you do: This simple activity is very educational and is also an activity that children enjoy doing for long periods of time. Simply provide children with the above materials and let them cut out pictures and glue them onto paper using the glue sticks.

This activity can also help children learn how to categorize and sort. Have the children cut out pictures, then sort them into specified categories, such as, people, furniture, clothes, or food.

Marvelous Miscellaneous Art Experiences

Frozen paint

This is a unique painting experience for young children. Just make sure that no one tries to taste the frozen paint!

ice cube paint

you will need: ice cube tray
food coloring
craft sticks
paper

extra tips

TiP 1: Also try painting on coffee filters.

what you do: Fill an ice cube tray with water. Add both food coloring and a craft stick to each ice cube tray section. Place in the freezer until the colored water is frozen. Provide the child with paper and the frozen paint. Let the child move the "popsicle-like" frozen paint around the paper.

frozen rainbow paint

you will need: ice cube tray
liquid tempera paint
craft sticks
paper

what you do: In an ice cube tray, add a shallow layer of tempera paint and a craft stick to each of the ice cube sections. Place in the freezer until the first layer is becoming frozen. Then add another layer of a different colored paint and so on, until there are four to five layers of paint in each ice cube section.

Provide the child with paper and the frozen paint and let the child paint. As this paint begins to melt, the colors will become more and more intense.

straw and string Art

The children will love both of these art experiences. Dipping string and moving it through the folded paper is fun. It is also exciting to open the folded paper to discover what happened when the string was pulled out! Watching the colors move and the paint "dance" around the paper when the children perform the super straw painting activity is equally as exciting.

silly stringy Art

you will need: liquid tempera paint
paper cups
paper
string or yarn

what you do: Lay a piece of paper on the table. Fold it in two and open it again. Prepare several colors of paint and pour them into small paper cups. Dip a piece of string into one of the colors of paint and place it on one-half of the paper. Fold the paper over the string, then pull out the string. Open the paper. Repeat with a new piece of string and a different color of paint. The effect of string art can be quite beautiful.

super straw painting

you will need: cake pan
paper
waxed paper
liquid tempera paint
plastic straws

what you do: Line a cake pan with waxed paper. Place a piece of white paper on top of the waxed paper.

Using a spoon, drip several drops of paint onto the paper. With the plastic straw, blow the paint around. This activity is great fun and it creates wild art!

Look what I made!

This was made by: